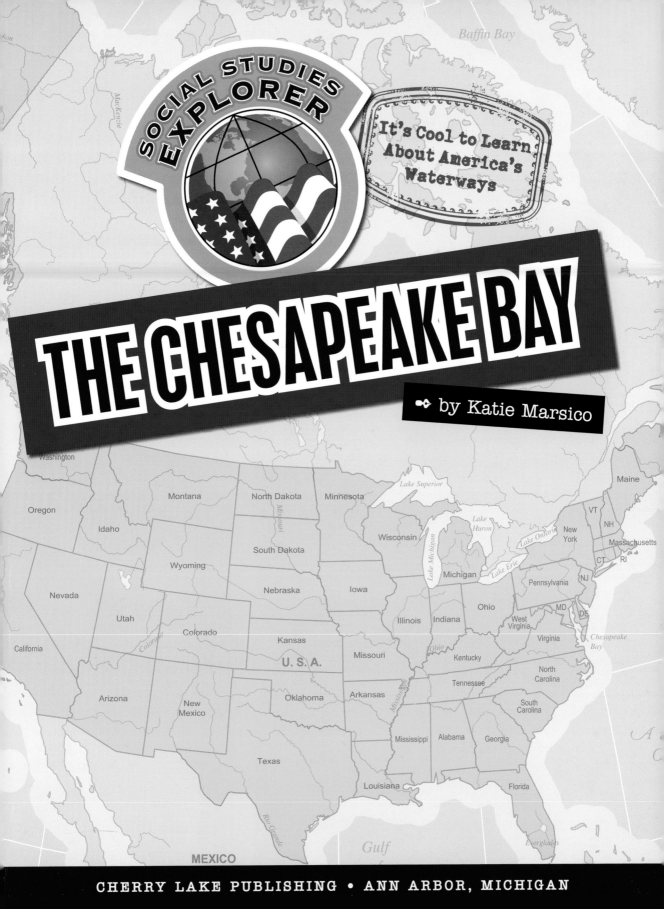

SOCIAL STUDIES EXPLORER

It's Cool to Learn About America's Waterways

THE CHESAPEAKE BAY

➤ by Katie Marsico

CHERRY LAKE PUBLISHING • ANN ARBOR, MICHIGAN

Published in the United States of America
by Cherry Lake Publishing
Ann Arbor, Michigan
www.cherrylakepublishing.com

Content Adviser: James Wolfinger, PhD, Associate Professor,
History and Teacher Education, DePaul University, Chicago, Illinois

Book Design: The Design Lab

Photo Credits: Cover and page 3, ©FloridaStock/Shutterstock, Inc., ©C.
Kurt Holter/Shutterstock, Inc., ©Lone Wolf Photos/Shutterstock, Inc.,
©Caitlin Mirra/Shutterstock, Inc., ©AlexanderZam/Shutterstock, Inc.;
Back cover and page 3 ©Apaterson/Shutterstock, Inc.; pages 4, 9, 12,
13, 14, and 16, ©Lone Wolf Photos/Shutterstock, Inc.; page 5, ©+F60
Ken Cole/Dreamstime.com; page 6, ©S.Borisov/Shutterstock, Inc.; page
7, ©iStockphoto.com/crossroadscreative; page 8, ©Jeremy Beeler/
Shutterstock, Inc.; page 10, ©Cameron Pickford/Dreamstime.com; page
18, ©Ilene MacDonald/Alamy; page 19, ©AP Photo/Jacquelyn Martin;
pagea 21 and 23, ©Edwin Remsberg/Alamy; page 22, ©COMO100670/
Media Bakery; page 26, ©Richard Ellis/Alamy; page 28, ©AUR0000938/
Media Bakery.

Library of Congress Cataloging-in-Publication Data
Marsico, Katie, 1980–
    The Chesapeake Bay / by Katie Marsico.
       p. cm. — (It's cool to learn about America's waterways)
    Includes bibliographical references and index.
    ISBN 978-1-62431-013-3 (lib. bdg.) — ISBN 978-1-62431-037-9 (pbk.) —
ISBN 978-1-62431-061-4 (e-book) 1. Chesapeake Bay (Md. and Va.) —
Juvenile literature. I. Title.
    F187.C5M37 2013
    551.46'1347—dc23   2012034740

Cherry Lake Publishing would like to acknowledge the work
of The Partnership for 21st Century Skills. Please visit
www.21stcenturyskills.org for more information.

Printed in the United States of America
Corporate Graphics Inc.
January 2013
CLSP12

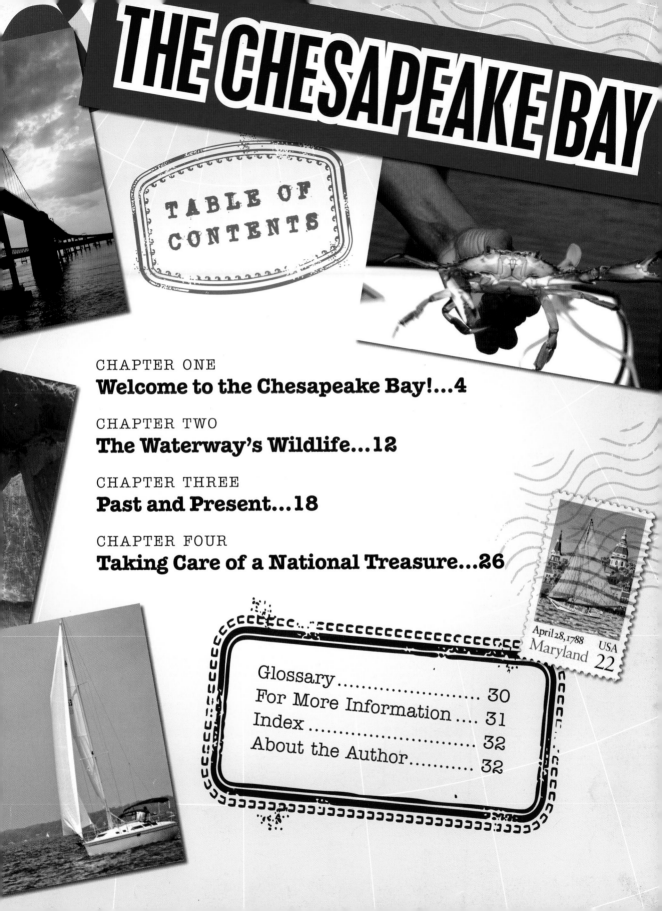

THE CHESAPEAKE BAY

TABLE OF CONTENTS

April 28, 1788   USA
Maryland 22

CHAPTER ONE

WELCOME TO THE CHESAPEAKE BAY!

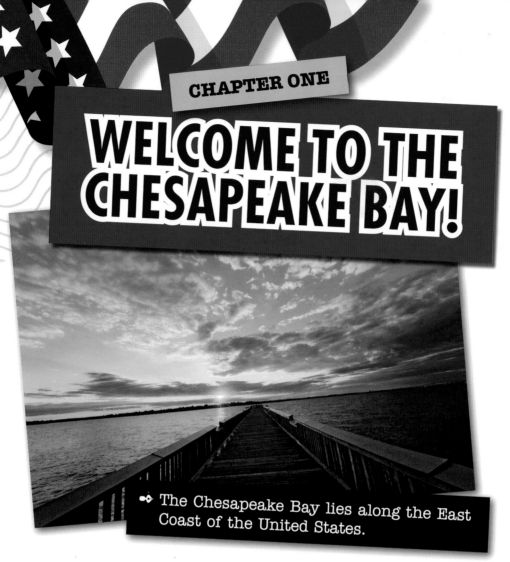

➻ The Chesapeake Bay lies along the East Coast of the United States.

Are you ready to have an adventure at the Chesapeake Bay? The bay is the largest **estuary** in North America. But this fact is only part of what makes it such an amazing and unique waterway. As you explore the Chesapeake Bay, you will spot a wide variety of wildlife, ranging from bald eagles to leather-back sea turtles. You will learn about melting **glaciers**, English explorers, and oyster reefs. During your journey, you'll get a few lessons in local culture and **cuisine**—which of course means sampling a serving of crab cakes! Yet your tour of the Chesapeake Bay will involve far more than trying tasty new

foods. By the time you leave, you'll have discovered why this waterway is an American treasure. It deserves your respect and protection.

Before you travel, it's important to map out exactly where you are going. The Chesapeake Bay is a large inlet, or arm, of the Atlantic Ocean. It stretches almost 200 miles (322 kilometers) between the Atlantic and the **mouth** of the Susquehanna River. The bay covers an area of roughly 1,700 square miles (4,403 sq km) near Maryland and approximately 1,500 square miles (3,885 sq km) near Virginia.

Jot down a few other facts about the waterway you will be visiting! The Chesapeake Bay measures about 30 miles (48 Km) at its widest point, near Cape Charles, Virginia. It is an average of 21 feet (6.4 meters) deep in most spots. The deepest portion of the bay is located southeast of Annapolis, Maryland. This area has depths of more than 170 feet (52 m). Finally, scientists estimate that the Chesapeake Bay contains a whopping 18 trillion gallons (68 trillion liters) of water!

➤ The Potomac River flows through Washington, D.C., and into the Chesapeake Bay.

Depending on how much time you have, your Chesapeake Bay adventure could take you into several other states as well. This is because the bay has more than 100,000 tributaries. A tributary is a river or stream that flows into a larger body of water. The Chesapeake Bay's main tributaries are the Susquehanna, Potomac, James, Rappahannock, and York Rivers.

The many waterways that pour into the bay—as well as the land surrounding them—form an extremely large **watershed**. A watershed is the region that drains a body of water and all of its tributaries. The Chesapeake Bay watershed measures 64,000 square miles (165,759 sq km). It includes portions of Maryland, Virginia, Delaware, Pennsylvania, New York, and West Virginia, and all of Washington, D.C.

CHESAPEAKE BAY MAP

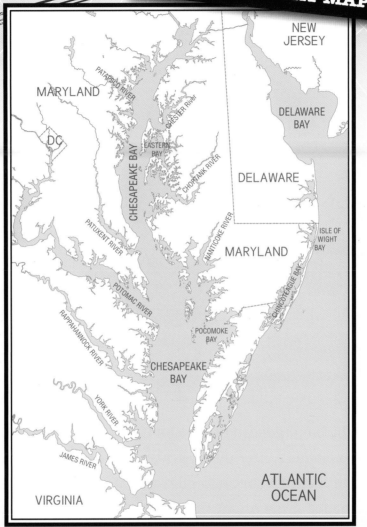

Take a few minutes to study this map of the Chesapeake Bay. Then lay a separate piece of paper over it and trace the waterway's outline. Label the Susquehanna, Potomac, James, Rappahannock, and York Rivers. Label the Atlantic Ocean, too. Mark your map with any other important locations you read about as you continue your journey!

STOP
Don't write in this book!

➤ The Susquehanna River is one of the many rivers that carry freshwater into the Chesapeake Bay.

You might have guessed that the Chesapeake Bay **ecosystem** includes many different types of **habitats**. When you visit, you'll travel through lush woodland areas where trees and shrubs grow along the water. You will also explore the Susquehanna, Potomac, James, Rappahannock, and York Rivers. Along with their hundreds of thousands of tributaries, these rivers are the source of nearly 90 percent of the bay's freshwater. (The upper portion of the Chesapeake Bay generally contains freshwater. Its lower section is filled with saltwater. You will find brackish water—a combination of freshwater and saltwater—in the middle.)

The Chesapeake Bay also features tidal marshes and thick beds of underwater grass. Shallow coastal areas border the shore. Stretches of open water and bay islands make up part of the local ecosystem, as well. You'll soon learn how important the health of these habitats is. It affects everything from countless species of wildlife to America's **economy**. In the meantime, start thinking about what you plan on putting in your suitcase!

Many species of waterbirds, such as the blue heron, live in the area surrounding the Chesapeake Bay.

● The Chesapeake Bay's beaches are especially fun to visit during the warm summer months.

Should you pack a sweater or a swimsuit for your adventure through the Chesapeake Bay region? Your choice of clothes will depend on when you're traveling and where you're visiting. What if you're heading to the northern portion of this waterway? For example, you might visit near the mouth of the Susquehanna River. There, you will likely experience hot summers and cold winters. Weather tends to be about 7 to 10 degrees Farenheit (3.8 to 5.5 degrees Celsius) warmer in southern sections of the bay. These areas are closer to the Atlantic Ocean. This half of the Chesapeake Bay typically features a more subtropical climate. In other words, it has milder temperatures in winter but more overall humidity, or dampness in the air, through the entire year.

Whether or not you should bring an oversized water bottle—or a raincoat—can also be difficult to decide. Both **droughts** and periods of heavy rainfall and flooding affect the Chesapeake Bay region. It's always wise to check the local weather forecast before you leave for a trip. Hopefully your journey will be filled with nothing but sunny skies and gentle bay breezes! Besides, you need to consider more than climate as you continue packing.

If you plan on swimming in the bay, be aware of the water temperature! The season and specific area you are visiting both affect how warm or cold you'll be. In general, though, water temperatures in the Chesapeake Bay range from around 34°F (1.1°C) to 84°F (28.9°C).

April 28, 1788 USA
Maryland 22

CHAPTER TWO

THE WATERWAY'S WILDLIFE

➥ The wildflowers that grow in the Chesapeake Bay area attract many different species of butterflies.

Be sure to tuck a pencil and a notebook in your suitcase. These items will come in handy if you want to keep track of the roughly 3,600 species of wildlife found in Chesapeake Bay habitats. This number includes about 2,700 types of plants that grow within the bay's ecosystem.

At least 50 species of trees exist in the Chesapeake Bay's watershed. Bald cypresses, Atlantic white cedars, and shadbushes are just a few types. Hundreds of colorful flowers bloom throughout the area as well. Think about bringing a camera with you. Then you can capture some images of yellow seaside goldenrod or pinkish-purple joe-pye weed. You will also spot cattails, cordgrass, and wild rice. Underwater grasses such as redhead grass, muskgrass, eelgrass, sago pondweed, and wild celery make up the bay's ecosystem, too.

Plants play a very important role in keeping local habitats clean. In some cases, their roots actually filter, or remove, chemicals from both underground and surface water. This limits how much pollution flows into the bay. Many plants also release oxygen into the water. This supports a healthy ecosystem because most living things need oxygen to survive.

◆◇ In autumn, leaves on trees surrounding the Chesapeake Bay turn shades of red and orange.

You may have a pet goldfish at home. But chances are you've never come face-to-face with a pumpkinseed or an American shad! These are only two of the more than 350 species of fish that swim through the Chesapeake Bay waters. Some, including the American shad, can live in both freshwater and saltwater habitats. The bay is also home to many types of crabs, including blue crabs, fiddler crabs, hermit crabs, horseshoe crabs, and marsh crabs. Keep your eyes peeled for shrimp, clams, jellyfish, and **mollusks**, too.

➥ Crabs are often found crawling along the shore of the Chesapeake Bay.

April 28, 1788
Maryland   USA
22

The Chesapeake Bay is especially famous for its oysters. These marine mollusks have rough, irregular shells. They play an important part in keeping the bay healthy. They feed by pumping large amounts of water through their breathing organs. This filtering process traps the tiny plants and animals that make up an oyster's diet. It also cleans the water by removing polluting substances. Communities of oysters used to form huge underwater reefs in the Chesapeake Bay. Unfortunately, overfishing, pollution, and disease have destroyed many of these habitats—and much of the local oyster population.

Hundreds of different kinds of birds are found in the Chesapeake Bay. Pack your binoculars so you can watch for ducks, geese, pelicans, plovers, egrets, herons, and ospreys. Also be on the lookout for hummingbirds, chickadees, and cardinals. If you're lucky, you might even glimpse a bald eagle or a wild turkey!

● Herons and other seabirds search the Chesapeake Bay for fish to eat.

Try searching the mouth of the Chesapeake Bay. You might spy one of the four species of sea turtles that are often sighted there. Some visitors even spot bottlenose dolphins playing in the middle and lower sections of the bay in the summer. This is also when people occasionally see manatees swimming through the waterway's shallow areas.

If you prefer touring nearby forests, have your camera ready. You could snap photos of bobcats, beavers, otters, deer, and foxes. For the moment, though, you had better close your suitcase and hit the road. Remember, watching wildlife is just one of many activities that will keep you busy around the Chesapeake Bay!

Make Your Very Own Field Guide

Have you ever heard of a field guide? This type of book describes the different plants and animals you are likely to find within a certain environment. Creating your own field guide is the perfect way to stay organized during your adventure! Simply pick 20 species of wildlife (or more if you want). Write the name of each one on a separate sheet of paper. Then prepare to do a little detective work on the computer or at your local library. Figure out—and record—the following information for all the plants and animals you have chosen:

Type of plant/animal (tree, shrub,
  flower/reptile, mammal, fish):
Habitat:
Appearance:
Other interesting facts:

    Print out or draw pictures of the species that you plan to include. Finally, make a cover and staple your pages together (or snap them into a binder). Don't forget to bring your guidebook along when you visit the bay!

CHAPTER THREE

PAST AND PRESENT

➡ The flooding of the Susquehanna River valley led to the formation of the Chesapeake Bay.

You're so close to the Chesapeake Bay that you can almost hear the sound of waves, seabirds, and honking ship horns. Yet you need to take a little detour before you officially reach your destination. You will still be visiting the bay. You'll just be traveling 18,000 years back in time to get there. That's when scientists believe the Chesapeake Bay started to form. Its formation began when melting glaciers flooded the Susquehanna River valley. It took 15,000 years of changes to the landscape before the bay looked similar to the body of water you will soon explore.

Human beings have a long history in what is now the Chesapeake Bay region. People may have even been present when the glaciers began melting! Over the centuries, many different American Indian groups settled in areas near the bay.

Beginning in the 1500s, European explorers entered the Chesapeake Bay. In later years, Great Britain claimed control of the waterway and settled much of the land around it. The bay became U.S. territory following the American Revolutionary War (1775–1783).

The Chesapeake Bay plays an important role in America's economy. Fishers **harvest** clams, oysters, and blue crabs there. Hunting, tourism, farming, and shipping are also big businesses in the region.

↩ Fishing in the Chesapeake Bay contributes to the region's economy.

19

ACTIVITY

TEST YOUR KNOWLEDGE

How much do you know about Chesapeake Bay history? Test your knowledge with the matching activity below. On the left side, you'll see the names of five people who were somehow connected to the Chesapeake Bay. On the right side, you'll see a description of the reasons these individuals are famous. Try to match each person with the correct description!

1) John Smith

A) Former slave who used escape routes along the bay to help Southern slaves flee to freedom in the North

2) Pocahontas

B) Born in Baltimore, Maryland, one of the greatest baseball players in history, he was affectionately known as "Babe"

3) Harriet Tubman

C) Powhatan noble who befriended early English settlers in the Chesapeake Bay region

4) Francis Scott Key

D) English explorer who visited and mapped the Chesapeake Bay between 1607 and 1609

5) George Herman Ruth

E) Author of the U.S. national anthem who witnessed American forces defend Baltimore against British troops stationed in the Chesapeake Bay in 1814

Answers: 1) D; 2) C; 3) A; 4) E; 5) B

STOP
Don't write in
this book!

About 17 million people live in the Chesapeake Bay watershed. About 59 percent of them live along or near the shores of the bay. Major cities in the watershed include Baltimore, Maryland; Norfolk, Virginia; and Washington, D.C. You can explore these and other areas now that you've finally arrived at the Chesapeake Bay!

What should you do first? If you want to enjoy a little beach action, head to Sandy Point State Park in Annapolis, Maryland. Swimming, canoeing, and hiking are all popular activities there. Another option is to check out Concord Point Lighthouse in Havre de Grace, Maryland. It was built in 1827 and is the oldest lighthouse in the state that is open to the public.

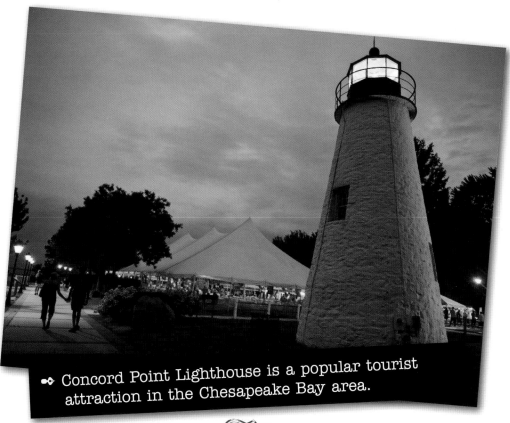

↤ Concord Point Lighthouse is a popular tourist attraction in the Chesapeake Bay area.

⚓ The history of Norfolk, Virginia, dates back to 1682.

Keep in mind that Virginia also borders the bay. If you'd like a guided tour of the waterway, you can book a ferry or riverboat cruise in Norfolk. Or, if you'd prefer to do a bit of bird-watching, spend a day at the Eastern Shore of Virginia National Wildlife Refuge near Cape Charles. Before you leave, remember to take a stroll along the refuge's butterfly and nature trails.

At some point during your Chesapeake Bay adventure, set aside time to sample the local cuisine. You'll find that many restaurants feature seafood dishes such as crab cakes and oyster stew. Clams, shrimp, and fresh fish are also popular dishes

on Chesapeake Bay menus. Finally, no dining experience in the bay would be complete without a delicious slice of Smith Island cake. This sweet treat is made from 6 to 12 extremely thin layers of yellow cake that are coated with rich chocolate frosting.

After dessert, you have to start packing up to go home. Before you say good-bye to the bay, however, prepare to think about a rather serious subject. By now, you probably realize that the Chesapeake Bay is a national treasure. As your journey nears an end, you need to consider what role you can play in protecting it!

Smith Island cake is an extremely popular example of Chesapeake Bay cuisine.

When people think of dining along the Chesapeake Bay, crab cakes are often one of the first foods to pop into their minds. Luckily, you don't have to be visiting America's largest estuary to enjoy a serving of this seafood dish! You can easily cook crab cakes at home—as long as you have an adult help you slice and dice the ingredients and operate your stove.

Quick and Easy Crab Cakes

INGREDIENTS

$\frac{1}{4}$ cup green onions

$\frac{1}{4}$ cup red bell pepper

One egg

Two 6-ounce cans of crabmeat

1 cup seasoned bread crumbs

$\frac{1}{4}$ cup low-fat mayonnaise

1 tablespoon lemon juice

$\frac{1}{2}$ teaspoon garlic powder

$\frac{1}{8}$ teaspoon cayenne pepper

1 tablespoon butter

INSTRUCTIONS

1. Chop the green onions and red pepper into fine, or very small, pieces. Place these vegetables in a bowl.

2. Beat the egg with a whisk or fork. Pour it into the bowl with the vegetables.

3. Add the crabmeat, bread crumbs, mayonnaise, lemon juice, garlic powder, and cayenne pepper to the mix. Stir the ingredients together.

4. Divide your mixture into eight pieces. Shape these portions into balls that are roughly 2 inches (5.1 centimeters) in diameter. (In other words, each crab cake should be slightly larger than a golf ball.) Flatten the balls until they are about 0.5 inches (1.3 cm) thick.

5. Warm the butter in a large nonstick skillet on your stovetop. Once the butter starts to simmer, use a spatula to gently drop the crab cakes in the pan. Cook them for 3 to 4 minutes on each side, or until they turn golden brown. Let the crab cakes cool before treating your dinner guests to a taste of the Chesapeake Bay!

CHAPTER FOUR

TAKING CARE OF A NATIONAL TREASURE

➡ Scientists often cast nets to catch fish in the Chesapeake Bay to test the animals for diseases.

Will your next trip to the Chesapeake Bay be as wonderful as the one you just experienced? It's hard to tell. This American waterway has changed over time—and not always for the better.

Runoff from nearby farms, factories, towns, and cities pollutes the Chesapeake Bay. Overfishing and overhunting have also created problems within the local ecosystem. In addition, people have developed approximately 4.4 million acres (1.8 million hectares) of the Chesapeake Bay watershed. The result is that many of the natural habitats there have been destroyed.

GRAPHING THE CHESAPEAKE BAY'S WATERSHED

Experts believe that during the 1600s, forests covered about 95 percent of the Chesapeake Bay's watershed. Today, that number has been reduced to roughly 58 percent. Approximately 23 percent of the land in the watershed is used for farming. People have developed 9 percent of the area into cities and suburbs. The remaining 10 percent of the bay's watershed is made up of mixed open spaces that include grassy areas such as golf courses.

Create a bar graph showing the breakdown of land use in the Chesapeake Bay's watershed today. Which bar do you predict will be the longest? Can you guess which one will be the shortest?

```
Land use in the Chesapeake Bay watershed
100
 90
 80
 70
 60
 50
 40
 30
 20
 10
  0
     Forests    Farming   Cities/Suburbs   Grassy areas
```

Fortunately, Americans like you can help save the Chesapeake Bay! Scientists, politicians, and average citizens are teaming up to support **conservation** efforts in the bay and its watershed. Part of their plan to restore the local ecosystem involves developing wildlife refuges. These areas protect threatened and endangered species from any human activity that might further decrease their numbers.

What can you do to encourage conservation of the Chesapeake Bay? Educate the public! Share all that you have learned during your adventure with family and friends. Discuss why the bay is such a remarkable American waterway—and how you can guarantee that it remains a national treasure for years to come.

By taking care of the Chesapeake Bay, you help ensure that people will be able to enjoy it long into the future.

ACTIVITY

WRITE A LETTER

THE CHESAPEAKE BAY

Political leaders in Maryland, Virginia, New York, West Virginia, Delaware, Pennsylvania, and Washington, D.C., are able to influence the future of the Chesapeake Bay. Together with other politicians across America, these men and women vote on laws and government projects that affect America's waterways. Writing a letter to such individuals makes them aware that people like you care about the bay. Ask an adult to help you find the addresses of officials who support conservation efforts. Then create a short, simple letter using the following outline:

Dear [INSERT THE NAME OF THE POLITICIAN(S) YOU DECIDE TO WRITE TO]:

I am writing to ask for your help in protecting the Chesapeake Bay. The bay is important to me because [INSERT TWO OR THREE REASONS THE BAY MATTERS TO YOU].

Thanks for your efforts to support this amazing American waterway!

Sincerely,

[INSERT YOUR NAME]

STOP
Don't write in this book!

GLOSSARY

conservation (kahn-sur-VAY-shuhn) the protection of valuable things, especially wildlife, natural resources, forests, or artistic or historic objects

cuisine (kwi-ZEEN) a style or manner of cooking or presenting food

droughts (DROUTZ) long periods without rain

economy (i-KAH-nuh-mee) the system of buying, selling, making things, and managing money in a place

ecosystem (EE-koh-sis-tuhm) all the livings things in a place and their relation to the environment

estuary (ES-choo-er-ee) the part of a river where it joins the ocean

glaciers (GLAY-shurz) slow-moving masses of ice found in mountain valleys or polar regions

habitats (HAB-uh-tats) places where an animal or a plant naturally lives

harvest (HAHR-vist) to gather crops that are ripe or animals that will be used as food

mollusks (MAH-luhsks) animals with a soft body, no spine, and usually a hard shell that live in water or a damp habitat

mouth (MOUTH) the part of a river where it joins the ocean or other large body of water

runoff (RUN-off) rainfall that is not absorbed by the soil and instead runs into streams and rivers

watershed (WAH-tur-shed) the region or land that drains into a river or lake

BOOKS

Johnston, Joyce. *Maryland*. Minneapolis: Lerner, 2012.

Rosenberg, Pam. *Watershed Conservation*. Ann Arbor, MI: Cherry Lake Publishing, 2008.

WEB SITES

Chesapeake Bay for Kids
www.chesapeakebayforkids.org
This Web site offers ideas and tips to young conservationists committed to saving the bay.

Maryland Department of Natural Resources (DNR)— Chesapeake Bay
www.dnr.state.md.us/Bay/education/kids.html
Learn more about local wildlife, as well as activities you can do to help restore the bay.

ABOUT THE AUTHOR
Katie Marsico has written more than 100 books for young readers. She hopes to visit the Chesapeake Bay in the near future. Ms. Marsico dedicates this book to her husband, Carl.